Equipped

Smart Catholic Parenting
in a Sexualized Culture

Foreword

We are living through a season of profound moral turbulence. Our young people are lost and are searching for purpose. They're looking for a way to make sense of the world and they desire to know the origin of their identity. This desire is written in each one of our hearts. Consider this:

Among young adults, 22% aged 18-24 consider porn to be good for society, and 8% of that age group think it is "very good for society." Further, when asked to prioritize what people consider immoral, teens and young adults consider "not recycling" to be more immoral than viewing pornography.

In an interview at the XIV Ordinary General Assembly of the Synod of Bishops on the Family (2015), where the synod fathers and I discussed the global dimensions of the problem of pornography, I explained:

> "Pornography's always been a problem. Ancient Rome was famous for it. Sex is powerful and fascinating, and people have always abused its appeal. But modern technologies make it a lot easier to access and much, much more widespread. It's an

epidemic; or more accurately a pandemic. Anyone with an internet connection anywhere in the world can find all the porn he or she wants. And note that word "she." Pornography used to be a largely male problem. Today, many women use it as well.

Porn does huge damage to families. It isolates individual family members by creating private sexual obsessions. And it wrecks the intimacy between husbands and wives with notions of "perfect" sex that bear no relation to real human beings. It's a terrible cheat. It steals the richness of a long term, mutually rewarding sexual friendship between husband and wife, and it substitutes a shabby replacement that can never really feed the human heart. [...] [P]orn also damages the larger family of the Church."

Pornography is a problem and is causing great confusion in our culture, marriages, homes and faith communities. Children are the most vulnerable; their brains are still developing and are most impressionable. Early sexual traumas can be an impetus for unhealthy sexual behavior later in life. Early inadvertent exposure can be the source of undeserved shame in a child. Children may keep from their parents the fact of exposure to pornography. They can believe the lie that it was their fault, and that both parents and God are unhappy. In this context, children can believe themselves to be dirty, unworthy, not lovable. All of which has the potential to reshape relationships with both parents and God and has implications for the whole of their lives.

Our young people need our guidance. They are eager for us to look up from our own smartphones and provide them with the attention and direction they need. Children can understand why God made them and what it means to be created in God's image. They can experience their own God-given dignity and the dignity of every person. By teaching our children the reason for their existence, we prepare them for the challenge to live in an overly sexualized culture.

What Equipped shows us is that by teaching our children about why God made them and what it means to be created in his image, we give the very reason for their existence. God created us in his image with great dignity and with a vocation to love and be loved. Equipped makes clear when we act on our own selfish desires, we do not live God's vision for us.

Equipped is both a theological and practical guide for parents on how to know and understand the origin and dignity of the human person. Equipped helps us to form, guide and protect children on matters of human sexuality and pornography, all in the light of Catholic teaching. An emphasis is put on Screen Accountability™ and Filtering – an offering provided through Covenant Eyes that I encourage every individual and family to consider. As you will read, internet accountability is key to overcoming the pornography pandemic and accountability is central to the life of true discipleship.

Again, Equipped provides parents with a Catholic resource on how to talk about God, sexuality and pornography. Discussing these topics can be overwhelming, and a shameful experience for parents who struggle themselves. I believe this book can begin the process of healing for adults too.

It's with great enthusiasm as your archbishop that I endorse Equipped and recommend it to the faithful of the Archdiocese of Philadelphia and beyond.

+ *Charles J. Chaput, ofm cap.*

Most Rev. Charles J. Chaput, OFM Cap.
Archbishop of Philadelphia
Chairman, USCCB Committee of Laity, Marriage, Family Life and Youth

Table of Contents

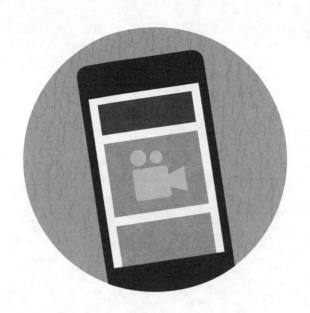

Getting Started

Covenant Eyes has created the *Safe Digital Family Challenge* to use with this book. To sign up, text SECURE to 66866. We'll wait....

All set up? Great! Now, let's begin.

01.

A House in Ruins

It is not an overstatement to say that in today's world, porn has become the norm.

The statistics are bleak and are trending in a disturbing direction—unless, of course, a massive culture shift begins today. Just ask the millennial generation—the first to grow up with Internet technologies in the home. Today, 79% of men in that generation say they watch pornography at least once a month (and most of these watch porn several times a week); 76% of women say they watch porn at least once a month.[1]

Pornography is powerful sexual education. It not only arouses: it leaves both young and old, men and women, wanting more of what they saw.

» 35% of boys reported viewing porn online "too many times to count."[2]

» 22% of young adults aged 18-24 consider porn to be good for society, and 8% of that age group actually think it is "very good for society."[3]

» When used to prioritize what people consider immoral, teens and young adults consider "not recycling" to be more immoral than viewing pornography.[4]

As a pediatrician for over 30 years and a consultant for the *National Center for Missing and Exploited Children*, Dr. Sharon Copper has seen the devastating impact pornography can have on the mind of a child. She explains pornography is neurologically more damaging to a child than to an adult for at least two reasons.[5]

1. **Children have an abundance of "mirror neurons" in their brains.** Mirror neurons convince us that when we see something we are actually experiencing it. When a man watches pornography, his mirror neurons activate, eventually triggering an erection because his body now believes it is experiencing sex.[6] With the abundance of mirror neurons in children, researchers believe this makes pornography more "real" to them.

2. **Children have an immature prefrontal cortex.**
   This is the area of the brain that controls judgement, controls impulses, and regulates emotion. This region of the brain isn't mature until it is between the ages of 20-22. Because children have such a weak prefrontal cortex, they lack the "executive control" to stop the flow of emotions and sensations that come from watching porn.

Parents are the Missing Link

Exposure to pornography is probably unavoidable for most people, but pornography problems are preventable. Be encouraged. As a parent, there are many steps you can take to not just protect kids but prepare them for a world without filters.

According to Dr. Patricia M. Greenfield, a researcher on sexual media at UCLA, the most important factor in reducing porn usage among teens is a warm and communicative parent-child relationship.[7]

02.

The Blueprint

The home and the family form the domestic church, which is "an image of God's love in human fellowship."[8] Thus it is the hub where we nurture our children into thriving adults who love the Lord with all their hearts, souls and minds— including how they steward their sexuality and others. Parents are the first educators, and are instructed by God to teach their children diligently "when you are at home and when you are away, when you lie down and when you get up" (Deuteronomy 11:19). It is no accident three of these four places—where our children live, where they wake, and where they sleep—are in the home.

It's easy to think that by setting a few parental controls that kids will be protected from digital risks. But this is simply not true! No amount of parental controls replaces the need for intentional formation from loving parents. Using the image of the home, this book presents some of the essential building blocks to prepare children for the overly sexualized culture kids will encounter on their screens and in the world around them.

The Four Walls: Self-Image, Sexuality, Sin, and Shame

Children must be given foundational truths about who they are, what sex is for and why it is good, the power and danger of misusing one's sexuality, and the trap of sexual shame. Within these four walls of truth, children are nurtured to become sexually integrated and healthy adults. Persistent, consistent, and loving conversations, even about the sometimes awkward topics of sex and human sexuality, are absolutely critical in order to form the hearts and the minds of our precious children.

Doors and Windows: Societal Messages

The doors and windows of a house show us the world outside—both the good and the bad. Wise parenting involves knowing when to open these digital doors, when to only allow our children to look through the glass, and when to bolt the doors and draw the curtains.

The Roof: Our Style of Parenting

The roof protects the home. A leaky roof makes the home a miserable place, no matter how well the walls are constructed. Our own virtuous character—the character of Christ in the home—covers our children with the kind of warmth and authority they need for their own character to be shaped into a virtuous life of self-giving.

The Foundation: The Security of the Teachings of the Catholic Church

When built on the sand, even a well-constructed home will eventually collapse. Without a secure foundation, even our walls of Sacred Scripture will look like moralistic pillars, and the roof of our best parenting intentions will feel disconnected and powerless. Our homes, therefore, need to be grounded in the teachings of the Catholic Church, which has its foundation and source in Sacred Scripture.

The teachings of the Catholic Church are good news! The Church extends a message of incredible optimism and joy. When that message is the bedrock of our homes, it grounds our children in something far more satisfying than the sexual messages of our culture. It grounds them in the goodness of the Triune God.

Have you put measures in place to guard the digital doorways in your home?

Sign up for the *Safe Digital Family Challenge* by texting SECURE to 66866.

03.

The First Wall

Porn sets up a false standard of beauty and worth—a false image of one's God-given identity and self-image. Indeed, porn is just the tip of a very large sexual media iceberg, constantly fueling us with a false message of beauty and worth. You don't even need to see pornography to be influenced by its values.

Preparing our children for the overly sexualized culture doesn't need to begin with conversations about intercourse, orgasms, or a tabloid story about the latest sex scandal. It should begin with instilling in our children

> You don't even need to see pornography to be influenced by its values

a sense of their God-given identity as a unique and unrepeatable person, and adopted son or daughter of God, which is the first "wall" of our structure.

Knowing They Are Created in God's Image

God is love![9] This has always been the case. Before time began, there was God the Father, God the Son, and God the Holy Spirit: a union of Persons and eternal exchange of life-giving love. God has destined humanity to share in this same eternal exchange of the love of the Trinity.[10, 11] This is at the very heart of being made in the image and likeness of God (Genesis 1:27). With this in mind, what does it mean for humanity to be created in "God's image"? Children need to be taught the answer to this question by starting with these foundational truths.

» Before time, there was God, whose very being is love.[12] God gave a beginning to all that exists outside of himself.[13] We know this event as creation. The Book of Genesis recalls the creation story when it states: "In the beginning...God created [us] in his image" as body-soul persons.[14, 15] By being made as a person (and both men and women possess the same dignity in the image of God), each of us reflects the Creator's wisdom and goodness. We are wholly unique and were granted intellect and free will, and therefore can decide for or against love.[16]

» Men and women are persons—not a some*thing*, but a some*one*. Men and women are critically objective. They can think beyond their immediate horizons, can work to improve their person, are aware of others as persons and understand their dignity, and can love others.[17]

» Men and women alone—and no other creatures— are "able to know and love his Creator."[18]

» In the beginning, God made man and woman to be givers and receivers of love. Patterned after God, men and women are designed to live in loving, sharing relationships with one another. We are responsible for one another.[19]

So what purposes were we designed for?

The Triune God, who is the perfect being and perfect community, created us out of the surplus of his love.[20] The world, including humanity—the pinnacle of God's creation—was made for God's glory. We are creatures of God's love. He wanted to share his boundless joy with us.[21, 22] He even established humanity in his friendship.[23]

Humanity is created by God and for God, and because of this, the desire for God is written in the human heart. The *Catechism of the Catholic Church* explains, "Of all visible creatures only man is "able to know and love his creator."[24] Thus, we "are here on earth in order to know and to love God, to do good according to his will, and to go someday to heaven."[25] Let's look at this more closely.

To know and to love God

If we are to love God and to serve him, we must first know him. How do we do this? We look to Sacred Tradition and Sacred Scripture. The *Catechism of the Catholic Church* states, "Scripture and Tradition never cease to teach and celebrate this fundamental truth: 'The world was made for the glory of God.'"[26]

Creation gives real witness to God's glory! As stated earlier, humanity is the pinnacle of God's creation. We are here to give witness to God's glory too! We do this by coming to know God through creation and revelation; by knowing our worth as his adopted sons and daughters

designed at the beginning of time and to know his will
and teachings spoken through the Church, including that
God made each of us to love him.

Love is a fundamental passion and it is aroused by
the attraction of the good.[27] The *Catechism of the Catholic
Church* defines love as "to will the good of another."[28] When
the Church says "God made us to love him," she means we
are invited to share in the love of the Blessed Trinity. Through
each of the Seven Sacraments, we are drawn deeper and
deeper into this communal life of the love of the Father,
Son, and Holy Spirit.[29]

To do good according to God's will

Creation manifests God's perfect love, as well as his goodness.
As mentioned earlier, creation is ordered towards God. He made
us and made us very good and with a purpose—to do "good"
and to "serve" God. In doing good, we serve God. By serving
God, each of us becomes the person God desires us to be.
When we choose not to serve God this is called sin. "The first
sin—the Original Sin of Adam and Eve—brought death and
suffering into the world. All of our sins—mortal or venial, major
or minor—have a similar though less drastic effect," though
still harmful.[30] When we sin, we harm our relationship with
God, family and community; we disturb the order of creation.[31]

To go someday to Heaven

God made each one of us for Heaven! He has always
willed us to be drawn into the very life of the Trinity—the
eternal exchange of love—and to enjoy eternal happiness
with him forever in Heaven. However, God gave us the
freedom to make the choice to accept his love and to
respond in love. In the Garden of Eden, we see man and
woman turn away from God's love and go their own way.[32]
Here humanity sins by denying God's plan for creation.[33, 34]
Today, when we choose to sin, we still deny him; we refuse
to love him in return and when we do this we reject all the
reasons why God made man and woman, we also reject
his plan for man and woman: "to go someday to heaven."[35]
According to Jennifer Messing from *Into the Deep*, who
speaks on the *Theology of the Body*, "This division of life-
giving Love affects the whole person, so we struggle with
both body and soul."[36] Even though we are no longer in the
Garden of Eden with the devil, the devil himself is "still subtle

and we still wander, but we are not defined by our sins or flaws. We never stop yearning for God (nor he for us)."[37]

When our children understand why God made them and what it means to be created in God's image, it impacts three main areas of their belief. They know:

1. **Your son or daughter possesses an inherent *dignity* that cannot be taken away from them.** The *Catechism of the Catholic Church* explains "The dignity of the human person is rooted in his creation in the image and likeness of God."[38] Man and woman are "the only creature[s] on earth that God has willed for [their] own sake," and [they] alone [are] called to share, by knowledge and love, in God's own life. It was for this end that [we were] created, and this is the fundamental reason for [our] dignity."[39] It is up to us, as parents, to instill in our children a sense of their great dignity in who they are and who God is calling them to be. God is their Creator; they are created in God's image. A reflection of God is found in all those he created, including your child personally. Your son or daughter shines forth a reflection of God himself. [40] To instill in our children a sense of their great dignity in who they are and who God is calling them to be:

- When you or your children hear
messages that promote only skin-deep
beauty, remind your son or daughter
that they are made in God's image as
the only creature called to share in God's
own life,[41] and that their dignity is based
on their identity as an adopted son or
daughter of God—and that is beautiful.

- Model for your children a positive
body image. While caring for our bodies
is good, obsessing over weight or our
physique is not.

- When something seductive appears
on the screen, turn your eyes away
and teach your children to do the same.
Have conversations with your children
about why you do this.

2. **They have a wonderful *destiny* that is preceded
by discipline and virtue.** Being created in God's
image includes with it an invitation and a calling
to both represent and share God with our
communities, society, and world. This sharing
and representation of God and the Gospel
message will come more naturally if your children
learn discipline and virtue, "an habitual and firm
disposition toward the good,"[42] early on in their

lives so as to not be inclined toward vices, which draw people away from the good.[43] This involves "educating our intellects to make good practical judgments and training our appetites to be subject to our intellects' judgements."[44]

- Continue to teach your children that the meaning of life is "to know and to love God, to do good according to his will, and to go someday to heaven."[45] The call to sexual purity and living out the virtue of chastity according to one's state in life is not running from pleasure, but running toward our ultimate fulfillment, which is found in obeying God. This brings us to communion with God, who gave us his commandments for our good (Deuteronomy 6:25).

- Resist the urge to praise your children in a way that labels them. Research shows when we praise children like this, *labeling* them as "smart" or "athletic" this does not give them confidence. Instead they become highly sensitive to failure.[46] Rather, focus on praising the *effort* they put forth. Commend them for when they seek discipline and virtue, including when they use their God-given gifts, talents, and energy wisely.

3. **Having failed to live the "Call to Love," they have a *Deliverer* who alone can make them whole.** Each one of us has a vocation to love. When our children fail and disobey—not *if* but *when*—it means they are falling short of the calling that God wrote into man and woman's identity back at "the beginning" of the story of Salvation History: to be givers and receivers of love. When we fall short of this call, we are missing the mark ("sin"), thus falling short of being God's image in the world. This is the bad news. The good news is that God doesn't abandon us in our sin, guilt, shame, or failure. God sent us a Rescuer and Redeemer to save us from our own sin and from eternal death. Messing says, "Jesus suffered in body and soul to atone for our physical and spiritual sins. We have been redeemed in body and soul by God's total gift of self: Love was poured out on the cross to heal our physical-spiritual division, making union with God (life in heaven) possible again!"[47]

> The good news is that God doesn't abandon us in our sin, guilt, shame, or failure

- Develop faith-based responses to your children's failings—even regarding sexual immorality. Rather than merely pointing out your disappointment in them, point them to our Lord. Explain: "I know what it's like to want to be unfaithful to God. But there's hope for people like you and me who struggle with infidelity." When we participate in the Sacrament of Reconciliation, God not only forgives us of our sins, he can even give us the grace to be faithful to him like never before.

- Develop planned, faith-based responses to sexual sin in the world. Use the message of our overly sexualized culture as an opportunity to draw the contrast to the message of Christ: "Do you see that? The world treats people like products to be purchased, sold, or disposed of according to our own selfish wishes. This is not how Jesus loves us. When Jesus died on the cross, his message was, 'This is my body given for you.' The message of all these sexual images we see is, 'This is your body taken by me.'"

Dignity. Destiny. Deliverer. This is what it means to be created and be recreated in the image of God. This is the first wall of truth that guards and guides the hearts, souls, and minds of our kids as they grow. But it is not the only wall.

04.

The Second Wall

It's not knowledge of the truth of our human sexuality according to God's design that scandalizes or robs our children of their innocence. It's the overall abuse of sexuality that does this.

In the first two chapters of Genesis, we see the three primary purposes for human sexuality in the context of marriage:

» **Sexuality is about the good of the spouses as well as the procreation of children.**[48] Marriage "render[s] mutual help and service to each other through an intimate union of their persons and actions."[49] The physical intimacy of spouses in the sexual embrace is not only for growing in love but it's also about the creation of new life—having children, the crowning glory of marital love.[50] "Married love itself is ordered to the procreation of children. After all, the first command given to Adam and Eve is "be fertile and multiply" (Genesis 1:28).[51] Sexual intercourse was designed by God to provide for spouses to further participate in God's ongoing design for creation.

» **Sexuality is a source of joy and pleasure for spouses.** The sexual embrace in marriage fosters self-giving and enriches greatly the joy, pleasure, and even gratitude of husband and wife.[52] God established that sexual intercourse in the context of marriage is pleasurable and enjoyable in both body and spirit.[53] Evidence of this comes from the first recorded words from Adam's mouth, a poetic celebration as he first lays his eyes on naked Eve, he proclaims: "This one, at last, is bone of my bones and flesh of my flesh" (Genesis 2:23). The pleasure in sexual intercourse helps create the unitive aspect of marriage.

» **Sexuality is for an intimate union of persons in marriage.** Sexual intercourse was designed by God to unify the couple even as far as spiritual communion. Sexual intercourse in marriage involves a total gift of self, a mutual self-giving and receiving. Married couples "give themselves definitively and totally to one another. They are no longer two; from now on they form one flesh."[54] The sexual act is "proper and exclusive to the spouses and it's not just biological but also concerns the innermost being of the persons."[55] During sexual intimacy, the neurochemicals oxytocin and vasopressin are released, laying down long-term memories in our cells, "binding" us to the memory of the source of the pleasure— our spouses.

Our brains control our sexuality, and also receive the deadliest blow from pornography.

When children view pornography, a region of the brain called the amygdala is activated, creating a sense of excitement, curiosity, and often anxiety. For boys, this anxiety is experienced as sexual tension, a desire to have the woman on the screen. For girls, this arousal is more "contextual," she desires to be the woman on the screen. Even young children experience these sensations—albeit in an underdeveloped way—and if left unchecked, these experiences can rewire the brain in startling ways.

Due to these neurological tendencies present in both boys and girls, it's absolutely critical for parents to talk openly and honestly about pornography in order to give children the words and tools they require to process what they see, and respond responsibly. Please visit **http://learn.covenanteyes. com/equipped-catholic/** for Parent Conversation Guides created by Covenant Eyes to guide parents in what to say and how to say it.

Porn robs us of givenness, life, pleasure, and oneness.

Givenness: God gives people to us and at the same time us to people. Every person, in some way, is a gift entrusted to us from God and vice versa. When God gifts others to us, he also tasks us with seeking and willing their good. In order to recognize every man or woman as the gift that he or she is, we must first give of ourselves in a sincere, total, and selfless way.[56] People are always a gift from God, and we are called to always make a gift of ourselves to others, including to our brothers and sisters, wives and husbands, friends, teachers and students.[57] Pornography does not communicate this givenness. Porn always teaches us to use and dispose of people and never to acknowledge that they are a unique and unrepeatable gift from God.

> Every person, in some way, is a gift entrusted to us from God

Life: Instead of being open to new life, pornography trains us to love solo-sexuality. Studies have shown that the more people view porn, the less they say they are attracted to the idea of marriage and having children. Over time, we come to prefer the cheap thrill of fantasy over the goodness of family.[58]

Pleasure: Rather than merely taking us to the heights of joy and pleasure through the life-giving sexual embrace in marriage, pornography causes our brains to fatigue, deadening us to real satisfaction. Continued exposure to porn releases surge after surge of dopamine, giving the brain an unnatural high. The brain eventually fatigues, damaging its pleasure receptors, leaving the viewer wanting more but unable to reach a level of satisfaction—unless they get more porn or more hardcore porn. This is called desensitization. Everyday pleasures begin to lose their luster—including sex —and the viewer expands his or her pornographic tastes to get the same level of arousal.[59]

Oneness: Instead of developing oneness with another person in the context of marriage, pornography bonds the viewer to an image. Studies have shown that when men and women are shown female centerfold models from pornographic magazines, it significantly lowers their judgments about the attractiveness of "average" people.[60] Behavioral therapist Andrea Kuszewski says the neurochemicals that fire when watching pornography "make you want to keep coming back to have that feeling," she says, and instead of wedding ourselves to a person, we wed ourselves to porn.[61]

Givenness. Life. Pleasure. Oneness. This is what human sexuality according to God's design is all about, and this is the very thing that pornography seeks to rob from the next generation. This is the second wall of truth that guards the hearts of our kids as they grow.

On the internet, porn is the norm. Learn how to protect your home by signing up for the *Safe Digital Family Challenge*.

Text SECURE to 66866 today!

05.

The Third Wall

The first two chapters of the Book of Genesis show us a world without sin. The last two chapters of the Book of Revelation show a new world, also without sin. Every chapter in between is a story of humanity prone to stray and a loving God rescuing us from our unfaithful ways.

The Book of Genesis offers us a picture into the hearts of Adam and Eve as they pluck the fruit from the tree of the knowledge of good and evil.

"The woman saw that the tree was good for food and pleasing to the eyes, and the tree was desirable for gaining wisdom.

So she took some of its fruit and ate it; and she also gave some to her husband, who was with her, and he ate it" (Genesis 3:6).

In the New Testament, Saint John the Apostle and Evangelist summarizes the events of the Garden of Eden in 1 John 2:16-17: "For all that is in the world, sensual lust, enticement for the eyes, and a pretentious life, is not from the Father but is from the world. Yet the world and its enticement are passing away. But whoever does the will of God remains forever."

Three desires pull at Eve's heart—the same three desires Saint John gives us in his summary of sin:

» The desire of the flesh ("the tree was good for food")—The word translated "desire" does not merely mean appetite or wish. It means over-drive, over-desire, or craving. The key idea here is *pleasure*.

» The desire of the eyes ("the tree was...pleasing to the eyes")—Again, the word used here is for a strong craving, but this time it is a drive to possess what one sees. The key idea here is *possessions*.

» The pride of life ("the tree was desirable for gaining wisdom")—Here, Saint John is speaking of arrogance and prideful ambition. The key idea here is *power*.

Pornography uses all three of these desires to tug at human hearts.

Pleasure: Our sexual drive is a God-given gift that has a context for life-giving union, but pornography is rocket fuel for the heart and mind—sex does the driving. Sex easily becomes an idol, consuming us and trumping all other concerns.

Possessions: Pornography treats women and men as trophies, mere objects to be collected and used instead of adored and appreciated.

Power: No longer do we need to work at cultivating real, holy relationships. Instead, pornography gives the illusion of control because every sexual fantasy is available with a click.

The story of the forbidden fruit helps us to see what the true enemies of our souls are—the devil and our own selfish passions. "Each person is tempted when he is lured and enticed by his own desire" (James 1:14).

Pleasure. Possessions. Power. We need to explain to our children that when we act on selfish desires, we do not live God's vision for us. The *Catechism of the Catholic Church* explains, "Only in the knowledge of God's plan for man can we grasp that sin is an abuse of the freedom that God gives to created persons so that they are capable of loving him and loving one another.[62]

Training our children to understand sin is crucial. Through our sins we miss the mark, abuse our freedom, and reject gifts God has bestowed. We haven't lived up to the standard of living we are called to in the Ten Commandments, the Two Great Commandments and the Beatitudes, which were given to us by God out of love. When we miss the mark and sin, we need to participate in the Sacrament of Reconciliation. It is there our Savior forgives us over and over again and we are reconciled with the Church—the community of faith we can harm.

06.

The Fourth Wall

No one taught Adam and Eve to feel shame. It was a response to what happens when created persons—men and women made in God's image—sin, and sin is not natural to man and woman. The *Catechism of the Catholic Church* explains, Adam and Eve were created in a state of holiness. Shame was a consequence of their personal sin and it affects all of humanity.[63]

If parents, who are prone to sin themselves because of the Fall, are going to guide their children, who are also impacted by sin and who also sin themselves due to the Fall, parents need to understand the purpose and power of shame and how to respond to it.

In reality, shame is not the enemy. Shame can, of course, become toxic when it is compounded by the belief that we are beyond the reach of grace, compassion, mercy and forgiveness. But the real enemy is our response to shame.

So let's look at shame from the perspective of what it means to have healthy shame: relational boundaries that remind us of the responsibilities of love. When loving communion is violated, the sense of shame is a call to return to authentic love. It is like an alarm that tells us something is not right with how we relate to others currently and calls us to return to how we should relate to them in love.

Now, with this understanding of healthy shame, let's look at what it is to have unhealthy or even toxic shame: It is the inability to receive love and mercy. It is the belief that one is fundamentally flawed and therefore unworthy of the gift of love. It is a distrust of the goodness of another that causes one to hide in distrust and fear (like Adam and Eve hiding from God in the Genesis story). This distrust and fear leads to autonomy from God (as opposed to trusting dependence on him), which leads to self-medicating or coping mechanisms, like pornography.

Therefore, shame is not always wrong, but it can become unhealthy and even toxic if it is distorted.

One of the most common ways parents encourage shame in their children is by using shame-based strategies to get their kids to behave. What exactly is "shame-based" parenting? It is a family dynamic where shame—the looming threat or presence of disapproval and disfavor—is the primary motivator used for good behavior. Expecting perfection. Speaking bitter or harsh words. Showing little compassion. Showing favoritism to other siblings.

Viewing Porn to Feel Better

Feeling Shame

Acting Out

Keeping it Secret

This kind of environment has unwittingly made so many childrenripe for sexually sinful habits.

When sexual sin is introduced to a child in a shame-based home, he or she is compelled to hide because there is no safety in being open and honest. Also, the chemical-fueled satisfaction that comes from viewing pornography gives comfort to a child who feels no warmth from his or her parents.

There are three primary ways children—all people, actually—deal with shame: hide, blame, and cover. We see these reflected in the Genesis story where Adam and Eve hide in the garden, blame the serpent, and cover their naked bodies.

As parents, what is the answer to the hide, blame, and cover response?

Fight Their Urge to Hide by Creating an Environment of Loving Accountability. An environment of accountability allows children to learn, explore, and even fail, but always with the expectation that mom and dad is present to guide, correct, and encourage.

Fight Their Urge to Blame by Fostering an Environment of Responsibility. Take time to instruct your children about the blame-shifting that happened in the Garden of Eden, then reinforce that lesson in the day-to-day life in the home. "Yes, someone said something mean to you online. But how did you react to that? What could you have done differently?"

Fight Their Urge to Cover by Reminding Them Christ Abolishes Our Sin. This means we, as parents, should make every effort to teach our children that Christ actually changes us at the level of our being, making us sharers in the divine nature (2 Peter 1:4). In the Sacrament of Reconciliation, Christ abolishes our sins. Thus, there is no need to try to cover up struggle and sin from God. He sees it all and wants your son or daughter to give their struggle and sin over to him in order to free them from it.

Jesus experienced the shame of our sin and the humiliation of being despised by men (Isaiah 53:3). He participated in our weakness. For this reason, he is our perfect rescuer and the one who sympathizes with our weaknesses. And even though we have sinned and continue to sin, he is not ashamed to call us brothers and sisters (Hebrews 2:11).

Shame is inevitable—not just about sexual matters, but all matters of our child's thoughts and behavior, both online and offline. The question is how we will prepare our children to understand shame and how to work through it in a healthy manner.

07.

Windows to the World

We are living at a dawn of an information revolution. Now that we have a few decades of Internet usage behind us, we are just starting to understand how media is positively and negatively impacting our lives.

Although the Internet is an amazing tool, pornography and technology has opened up new access points to our families. It creates windows and doorways that are difficult to guard and control because the Internet is knocking 24/7. It does not rest and it continues to present more invasive opportunities for the outside world to enter our lives.

When it comes to both online and offline threats, the fact remains there will probably always be people who seek to use others and not treat them as God-given gifts. Particularly, as a parent in the Internet age, it's important for you to acknowledge that pornography is damaging when seeking to understand, live and hold up the dignity of the human person and the beauty and goodness of human sexuality.

The *Catechism of the Catholic Church* defines pornography as "...removing real or simulated sexual acts from the intimacy of the partners, in order to display them deliberately to third parties. It offends against chastity because it perverts the conjugal act, the intimate giving of spouses to each other. It does grave injury to the dignity of its participants (actors, vendors, the public), since each one becomes an object of base pleasure and illicit profit for others. It immerses all who are involved in the illusion of a fantasy world. It is a grave offense."[64]

When it comes to protecting our kids from the worst of the worst on the Internet and through apps, an effective approach must be multi-faceted. This involves teaching your children about the topics we have covered thus far in this book: God-given identity, the importance of sexual integrity, the difference between sexual impulse and life-giving union and how to understand sexual shame, it must also include having healthy, balanced, open and honest conversations, while filtering out

> Its important to treat accountability not as a last resort but as a lifestyle

pornography, and constant monitoring of how they use their devices.

Screen Accountability™ software is a key component in forming and shaping your son or daughter to be the virtuous and integrated children they are called to be.

Accountability is one of God's ordinary means to help us become more like Christ. In the overall life of your family and as you educate and form your children, its important to treat accountability not as a last resort but as a lifestyle. When children are accountable to someone through Covenant Eyes Screen Accountability™, they will experience:

» Love, care, and protection

» Being known online and offline

» Vulnerability and openness without the fear of being discovered

From the age children start to use Internet-connected devices until their mid-teens, parental controls are very helpful for filtering and monitoring. No matter what tools or technology are used, parents should be upfront about these controls with their children.

Please visit the list of Resources at the end of this book. There you will find partners who help inform and educate parents on the latest devices, parental controls, and apps. Please take time to consider them—they are the best of the best.

When it comes to formation and education, literacy is more than the ability to read and write. Literacy is about comprehension and critical thinking skills. The same is true for media literacy: applying critical thinking skills to the media we consume.

Co-Viewing: Formation and education needs to start by viewing and/or listening to media with your children. Yes, this takes time, but it pays dividends.

Dialogue: Look your children in the eyes often and have consistent and persistent conversations about what they are experiencing when interacting with media. These open and honest conversations are key to cultivating accountability with your children and in the overall life of your family.

Unfortunately, we can't lock every digital door and prevent all media dangers from impacting our children. Therefore, the best defense is the internal filter in their mind and heart that they carry with them. Forming this defense takes time and intentionality. Using Covenant Eyes and engaging your children in conversations help create an accountable home and an overall culture of openness.

Covenant Eyes has created conversation guides for parents to use during the four primary stages of a child's life. These guides show parents the types of words and phrases they can use to prepare their kids for digital environments and the distorted pull of pornography. These conversation guides can be accessed at **http://learn.covenanteyes.com/equipped-catholic/.**

Over 300 hours of video are uploaded to YouTube every minute![65] Find out how to control YouTube with the *Safe Digital Family Challenge*.

To sign up, text SECURE to 66866.

08.

The Roof of Protection

A wise parenting style serves as a roof of protection for our kids. No matter what walls of formative teaching we construct or what windows of media usage are in place, the leaky roof or poor parenting makes the home a dangerous place to live.

To be wise fathers and mothers in the digital age, we need to grapple with God's timeless guidance and instruction to parents. Guidance and instruction that call us to strive for a balance between **structure** and **support**.

Discipline is all about structure. It involves managing one's household well (1 Timothy 3:4, 12) and training children not to be unruly (Titus 1:6) by warning (1 Corinthians 4:14), imploring (1 Thessalonians 2:11-12), correcting, and chastising (Hebrews 12:5-7).

STRUCTURE

	Demanding	Not Demanding
Responsive	Authoritative	Permissive
Not Responsive	Authoritarian	Neglectful

SUPPORT

Instruction is all about support. It involves opening your heart wide to your children in love (2 Corinthians 6:13), providing for them (Luke 11:11-13; 2 Corinthians 12:14), engaging them in encouraging and comforting dialogue (1 Thessalonians 2:11-12), and modeling what real virtue looks like (1 Peter 5:1-4).

Indulgent or *permissive* parents (all support, little structure) unwittingly train children to believe their every whim and desire is good. These parents baby their children, even into their young adult years, falsely believing the best way to nurture a child's character is through fewer rules and more love.

Then when sexual temptations come knocking, there's little in the child's character that would compel him or her to say no. If life is about my pleasure, if the world is meant to revolve around me and cater to my whims, then pornography is the ultimate sexual fantasy world to make them feel great.

On the other end of the spectrum, *legalistic* or *authoritarian* parents (all structure, little support) train children to seek refuge anywhere but at home. Obsessed with peak performance, these parents create an overly critical home devoid of affirmation and encouragement. Kids in these homes start to believe their parents don't care about them.

As a result, sex and porn provide the perfect fantasy world to feel a counterfeit version of love, affirmation, and power —a risk-free place where he or she isn't criticized, judged, or a disappointment to others. In other words, legalistic parents unwittingly chase their children into the minefield of sexual sin.

As far as we are able, parents ought to avoid these extremes and instead give our children the structure and support God instructs us to give them by being authoritative. This occurs when we have equal strength in our institutional and personal authority.

Institutional authority. This is the authority parents have simply by virtue of being parents. It is why God commands children to honor their parents.

Personal authority. This is the kind of authority parents have by taking responsibility, by showing love, attention, and affection. It is the kind of authority that is earned through personal devotion.

Institutional authority is like having your name on the checkbook. Personal authority is like having money in the bank. You can only get out of the account what you put in.

Which one best describes you? Ask yourself a few questions:

» Is your home a place where your kids have a clear sense of what you expect of them and what God expects of them?

» Are you having regular conversation with your kids about wise and virtuous living as they mature?

» Do you coach your children through their problems, teaching them to solve conflicts?

» Is your home a place where your kids feel affirmed, encouraged, and loved?

» Do you listen when your children have complaints or concerns?

A "no" response in any of these areas might point to an opportunity. Don't worry. Perfection isn't the goal. Make this your goal: "In each phase of the day when I interact with my own children, I will either be an example to them in my faithfulness to God, or I will be an example in how I return to God."

How do we work towards this balance of structure and support? To do this, we need to have homes grounded in a relationship with God. Spend time in prayer and with Sacred Scripture, participate in the Sacraments, individually and as a family. Have regular conversations about his presence in your daily lives. Keep your eyes on him. Consistently. Intently. Nothing is more important.

09.

The Foundation

Despite all the best parenting in the world, we will not protect our children from struggle and sin. Both are part of the human experience because of the Fall.

Because of the Fall, it is absolutely necessary to teach our children about their identity and appropriate boundaries, especially as it pertains to human sexuality, including their lives online and offline. But their greatest need in life in not a good understanding of sexuality, a good sexual track record, or even good parents—their greatest need in life is God, including an understanding of their adoption as his child, as well as his Divine Mercy.

In summary, the message of the Catholic faith that we need to give to our children is this. It is the message of the Gospel: Rejoice and be glad! God sent us his Only Son, the promised

King of the world, Jesus the Messiah. He came as a baby, just like each of us, and lived among us. He experienced real life! He had real happiness, real struggles, real friends, and real pain. Because of what he taught, people hated him and killed him. He died for our sins, just as the Bible said he would. But (this is the Good News!) three days later, this King rose from the dead, just as Sacred Scripture foretold! Because of what Jesus has done, we can be saved from the guilt of sin and finally have peace with God forever. Everyone! The sick and the healthy. We are his! We just need to keep our eyes on Jesus by living the Catholic faith, being close to him in prayer, participating in the Sacraments and announcing the Gospel of the Lord. When we do that, not only do we experience a full, amazing life now, but we also get to participate in the love of the Trinity for all eternity.

Weave this message into everyday conversation.

A child who understands that he or she has value because of Jesus—meaning they don't have to earn his love, but at the same time know they need to live in a way that corresponds to Jesus' love rather than violating it— is more likely to be a child who chooses to honor Jesus with their choices. Whether that be in their family and friendships, technology, sexuality, etc.

A performance-oriented home is centered on what kids do, but a home grounded in the Catholic faith is all about who Christ is and our identity in him. When the faith becomes central to our parenting, each act of disobedience from our kids can become an opportunity for us to point our children to Jesus.

The grace and mercy of God doesn't extend just to our children. It also extends to us as parents—and that is very good news. If our identity as a parent is grounded on a flawless parenting track record, we will quickly be driven to hyper-perfectionism, despair, or apathy. But if our parenting is grounded in Divine Mercy, then we know God's primary expectation of us is not our performance as a parent but our dependence on him.

As parents, nothing is more important than our belief in Divine Mercy, accompanied by participation in the Sacraments. Pray to God for a deep understanding of his Divine Mercy in your own life. For in the Gospel, in prayer, and in the Sacraments, we find the joy needed to parent well.

CovenantEyes™

THEIR PROTECTION IS IN YOUR HANDS
Protect Your Family from Internet Pornography

Parents today face increasing challenges in protecting their children's innocence. Pornography can enter the home through a variety of doors. Covenant Eyes Screen Accountability and Filtering can help parents monitor digital doors and teach their children to use technology well. While this could be an overwhelming task, Covenant Eyes has the resources you need to be the parent your children need.

CovenantEyes

Guide Your Children Online

Get the digital safety tips every parent and caring adult needs to know. Clean Heart Online is a one stop portal for families who want information about raising responsible digital natives. You'll also find information for adults who want to live online with integrity. It's all free!

https://CleanHeart.Online

CovenantEyes™

STRIV™

21-DAY DETOX FROM PORN

BE THE FATHER THEY NEED
Discover the keys to a life of integrity with STRIVE

Are you a father or young man struggling to overcome the compulsion to view pornography? Join the *Strive 21-Day Challenge* with Matt Fradd.

With your free registration, you'll recieve:

- Step-by-step plan with powerful videos and challenges delivered daily.

- Exclusive access to past, current, and future interactive live streams with Matt & special guests.

- Connect with brothers from around the world each day in the online community.

Register for FREE today
at Strive21.com

Resources

Clean Hearts Online

Clean Hearts Online is an educational website that provides resources **for clergy, parents, educators, and even those who struggle with pornography.** Available content includes video courses, online certification, information regarding local diocesan training workshops, local counselors and more.

cleanheartsonline.com

The Chastity Project

Chastity Project is a ministry of Jason and Crystalina Evert that promotes the virtue of chastity through seminars, resources, clubs, and social media.

http://chastityproject.com

Protect Young Eyes

Protect Young Eyes is a parental control and technology education organization founded by Internet Safety expert Chris McKenna, built especially for parents and caregivers. Their website explains how to monitor social media, how to make kids predator proof, how to identify screen time addiction, and so much more. The PYE presentation team also speaks at hundreds of schools every year.

www.protectyoungeyes.com

References and Notes

1. 2014 Pornography Survey and Statistics. Proven Men Ministries. http://www.provenmen.org/2014pornsurvey/ (accessed Dec. 29, 2014).

2. Bev Betkowski, "1 in 3 boys heavy porn users, study shows," *Eurekalert. org*, Feb. 23, 2007. https://heavy.eurekalert.org/pub_releases/2007-02/uoa-oit022307.php (accessed Dec. 9, 2013).

3. Barna Group, *The Porn Phenomenon: The Impact of Pornography In the Digital Age*, (Josh McDowell Ministry, 2016), 28.

4. Ibid, 53.

5. Sharon Cooper, M.D., "Pornography Harms Children," *Pornharms. com*, Video, 7:21, June 15, 2010, https:// www.youtube.com/watch?v=TFw1Cnuq9jc&feature=c4-overview-vl&list=PL9D96079D4DEDCE38 (accessed March 21, 2016).

6. Alison Motluk,"Mirror neurons control erection response to porn," *New Scientist*, June 16, 2008, https://www.newscientist.com/article/dn14147-mirror-neurons-control-erection-response-to-porn/ (accessed March 21, 2016).

7. Patricia M. Greenfield, "Inadvertent exposure to pornography on the Internet: Implications of peer-to-peer file-sharing networks for child development and families," *Applied Developmental Psychology* 25 (2004): 741- 750, https://www.eurekalert.org/pub_releases/2005-03/uoc--tfi030105.php (accessed March 21, 2016).

8. Christoph Cardinal Schönborn O.P., *Youth Catechism of the Catholic Church* (San Francisco: Ignatius Press, 2011), no. 271.

9. *Catechism of the Catholic Church* (2nd ed.) (Washington, D.C.: Libreria Editrice Vaticana [LEV] United States Catholic Conference of Catholic Bishops [USCCB], 2000, no. 221.

10. *Catechism of the Catholic Church* (2nd ed.) (Washington, D.C.: Libreria Editrice Vaticana [LEV] United States Catholic Conference of Catholic Bishops [USCCB], 2000, no. 221.

11. Messing, Jennifer. *Everyone's Story in Light of St. John Paul II's Theology of the Body*. Handout. Into the Deep. Minneapolis, Minnesota. 2015.

12. *Catechism of the Catholic Church* (2nd ed.) (Washington, D.C.: Libreria Editrice Vaticana [LEV] United States Catholic Conference of Catholic Bishops [USCCB], 2000, no. 221.

13. *Catechism of the Catholic Church* (2nd ed.) (Washington, D.C.: Libreria Editrice Vaticana [LEV] United States Catholic Conference of Catholic Bishops [USCCB], 2000, no. 290.

14. *Catechism of the Catholic Church* (2nd ed.) (Washington, D.C.: Libreria

Editrice Vaticana [LEV] United States Catholic Conference of Catholic Bishops [USCCB], 2000, no. 362-268.

15. Messing, Jennifer. *Everyone's Story in Light of St. John Paul II's Theology of the Body*. Handout. Into the Deep. Minneapolis, Minnesota. 2015.

16. Christoph Cardinal Schönborn O.P., *Youth Catechism of the Catholic Church* (San Francisco: Ignatius Press, 2011), no. 56.

17. Ibid, no. 58.

18. Ibid.

19. Christoph Cardinal Schönborn O.P., *Youth Catechism of the Catholic Church* (San Francisco: Ignatius Press, 2011), no. 122.

20. Ibid, no. 2.

21. Ibid.

22. Ibid.

23. *Catechism of the Catholic Church* (2nd ed.) (Washington, D.C.: Libreria Editrice Vaticana [LEV] United States Catholic Conference of Catholic Bishops [USCCB], 2000, no. 355.

24. Ibid, no. 356.

25. Christoph Cardinal Schönborn O.P., *Youth Catechism of the Catholic Church* (San Francisco: Ignatius Press, 2011), no. 1.

26. *Catechism of the Catholic Church* (2nd ed.) (Washington, D.C.: Libreria Editrice Vaticana [LEV] United States Catholic Conference of Catholic Bishops [USCCB], 2000, no. 293.

27. Ibid, no. 1765.

28. Ibid, no. 1766.

29. Scott Richert, "Why Did God Make Me?" *About.com*, October 31, 2015, http://catholicism.about.com/od/baltimorecatechism/f/Question_6_BC.htm (accessed October 18, 2016).

30. Ibid.

31. Ibid.

32. Messing, Jennifer. *Everyone's Story in Light of St. John Paul II's Theology of the Body*. Handout. Into the Deep. Minneapolis, Minnesota. 2015.

33. Scott Richert, "Why Did God Make Me?" *About.com*, October 31, 2015, http://catholicism.about.com/od/baltimorecatechism/f/Question_6_BC.htm (accessed October 18, 2016).

34. Messing, Jennifer. *Everyone's Story in Light of St. John Paul II's Theology of the Body*. Handout. Into the Deep. Minneapolis, Minnesota. 2015.

35. Christoph Cardinal Schönborn O.P., *Youth Catechism of the Catholic Church* (San Francisco: Ignatius Press, 2011), no. 1.

36. Messing, Jennifer. *Everyone's Story in Light of St. John Paul II's Theology of the Body*. Handout. Into the Deep. Minneapolis, Minnesota. 2015.

37. Ibid.

38. *Catechism of the Catholic Church* (2nd ed.) (Washington, D.C.: Libreria Editrice Vaticana [LEV] United States Catholic Conference of Catholic Bishops [USCCB], 2000, no. 1700.

39. *Catechism of the Catholic Church* (2nd ed.) (Washington, D.C.: Libreria Editrice Vaticana [LEV] United States Catholic Conference of Catholic Bishops [USCCB], 2000, no. 356.

40. John Paul II, On the Value and Inviolability of Human Life *Evangelium vitae*, 25 March 1995, http://w2.vatican.va/content/john-paul-ii/en/encyclicals/documents/hf_jp-ii_enc_25031995_evangelium-vitae.html (accessed 27 July 2017), no. 34.

41. Ibid.

42. Ibid, no. 1803.

43. Sister Therese Auer, O.P., *Called to Happiness: Guiding Ethical Principals* (Third Edition) (Nashville, Tennessee: Dominican Sisters of St. Cecilia Congregation, LBP Communications, 2013), p. 152.

44. Ibid, p. 154-155.

45. Christoph Cardinal Schönborn O.P., *Youth Catechism of the Catholic Church* (San Francisco: Ignatius Press, 2011), no. 1.

46. Ann Pleshette Murphy, Jennifer Allen, "Why Praise Can Be Bad for Kids," *ABC News*, Feb. 15, 2007, http:// abcnews.go.com/GMA/AmericanFamily/Story?id=2877896&page=1 (accessed March 21, 2016).

47. Messing, Jennifer. *Everyone's Story in Light of St. John Paul II's Theology of the Body*. Handout. Into the Deep. Minneapolis, Minnesota. 2015.

48. *Catechism of the Catholic Church* (2nd ed.) (Washington, D.C.: Libreria Editrice Vaticana [LEV] United States Catholic Conference of Catholic Bishops [USCCB], 2000, no. 2363.

49. United States Conference of Catholic Bishops (USCCB), *Marriage: Love and Life in the Divine Plan*, 2009, p. 12.

50. Ibid, p. 14.

51. Ibid.

52. *Catechism of the Catholic Church* (2nd ed.) (Washington, D.C.: Libreria

Editrice Vaticana [LEV] United States Catholic Conference of Catholic Bishops [USCCB], 2000, no. 2362.

53. Ibid.

54. Ibid, no. 2364.

55. Ibid, no. 2361.

56. John Paul II, *A Meditation on Givenness*, Communio International Catholic Review (Volume 41.4), 2014. http://www.communio-icr.com/files/jpii41-4.pdf, p. 874.

57. Ibid, pp. 871-872.

58. Dolf Zillmann and Jennings Bryant, "Effects of Prolonged Consumption of Pornography on Family Values," *Journal of Family Issues* 9 (4), 1988.

59. Gary Wilson, "The Great Porn Experiment," *TEDxGlasgow*, 2012. http://tedxtalks.ted.com/video/TEDxGlasgow-Gary-Wilson-The-G-2 (accessed June 16, 2014).

60. Raymond M. Bergner and Ana J. Bridges, "The significance of heavy pornography involvement for romantic partners: research and clinical implications," *Journal of Sex, Marital Therapy* 28 (3), 2002.

61. Davy Rothbart, "He's Just Not That Into Anyone," *New York Magazine*, last modified January 30, 2011, http://nymag.com/nymag/features/70976/index1.html (accessed March 24, 2016).

62. *Catechism of the Catholic Church* (2nd ed.) (Washington, D.C.: Libreria Editrice Vaticana [LEV] United States Catholic Conference of Catholic Bishops [USCCB], 2000, no. 387.

63. *Catechism of the Catholic Church* (2nd ed.) (Washington, D.C.: Libreria Editrice Vaticana [LEV] United States Catholic Conference of Catholic Bishops [USCCB], 2000, no. 398, 404.

64. *Catechism of the Catholic Church* (2nd ed.) (Washington, D.C.: Libreria Editrice Vaticana [LEV] United States Catholic Conference of Catholic Bishops [USCCB], 2000, no. 2354.

65. Danny. "37 Mind Blowing YouTube Facts, Figures and Statistics – 2018." MerchDope, April 26, 2018. Accessed June 1, 2018. https://merchdope.com/youtube-statistics/.

Contributors

Lead Writer | Amanda Zurface, JCL

Lead Writer | Luke Gilkerson

Designer | Rachael Moss

Editor | Chris McKenna

Editor | Lisa Eldred

Editor | Sam Guzman

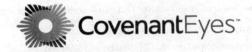

www.covenanteyes.com

1.877.479.1119

1525 W. King St., PO Box 637
Owosso, MI 48867